HOW THE FUTURE BEGAN

EVERYDAY LIFE

HOW THE FUTURE BEGAN

EVERYDAY LIFE

CLIVE GIFFORD

KINGFISHER

KING*f*ISHER

Kingfisher Publications Plc
New Penderel House,
283–288 High Holborn,
London WC1V 7HZ

Author
Clive Gifford

Senior Editor
Clive Wilson

Designer
Veneta Altham

DTP Co-ordinator
Nicky Studdart

Production Controller
Jacquie Horner

Picture Research Manager
Jane Lambert

Picture Researcher
Juliet Duff

Indexer
Hilary Bird

First published by Kingfisher Publications Plc 2000
(hb) 1 3 5 7 9 10 8 6 4 2

Copyright © Kingfisher Publications Plc 2000

A CIP catalogue record for this book is available from
the British Library.

ISBN 0 7534 0433 8 (hb)
1TR/0300/TWP/RNB/135NYMA

Printed in Singapore

CONTENTS

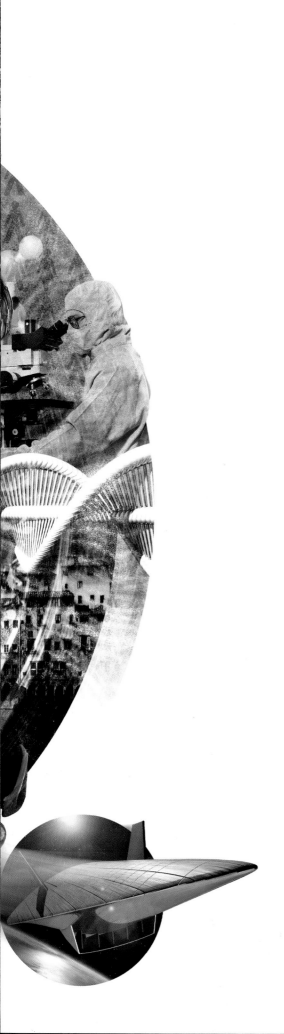

During the 21st century, we will witness great changes in our everyday lives. Breakthroughs in fields as diverse as medicine, communications, architecture and transport will have a major impact on society. Most people will live in cities, which will go on growing outwards and upwards. Inside your intelligent home, sensors will detect your presence and automatically adjust the environment. If you own a car, it will probably be a non-polluting electric model. For longer journeys, new forms of propulsion will massively cut the journey times for train, sea and air travel.

A range of new technologies will continue to power the Information Revolution. The next generation of Virtual Reality and holographic communication systems will have far-reaching effects on areas such as education and the way we work. Advances in healthcare and medicine will see a significant increase in life expectancy and, one day, gene therapy may even be able to prevent most life-threatening diseases.

Everyday life for people in developed countries will be safer and more productive than ever before. However, many important issues will still need to be addressed. These will include serious water and food shortages in many parts of the world, overcrowding in cities, pollution, traffic control and the consequences of an increasingly ageing population. Biotechnology and genetic engineering will benefit millions of people but concerns about the potential misuse of these new technologies are likely to continue for some time.

1999
Petronas Towers,
world's tallest
building, completed

1970s
Use of composite
materials

1934
Fluorescent light
invented

1931
Empire State
Building completed

1892
Reinforced
concrete invented

1885
First skyscraper
built in Chicago, USA

1779
Completion of first
all-metal bridge
in England

3500BC
First cities appear
in Mesopotamia
(now Iraq)

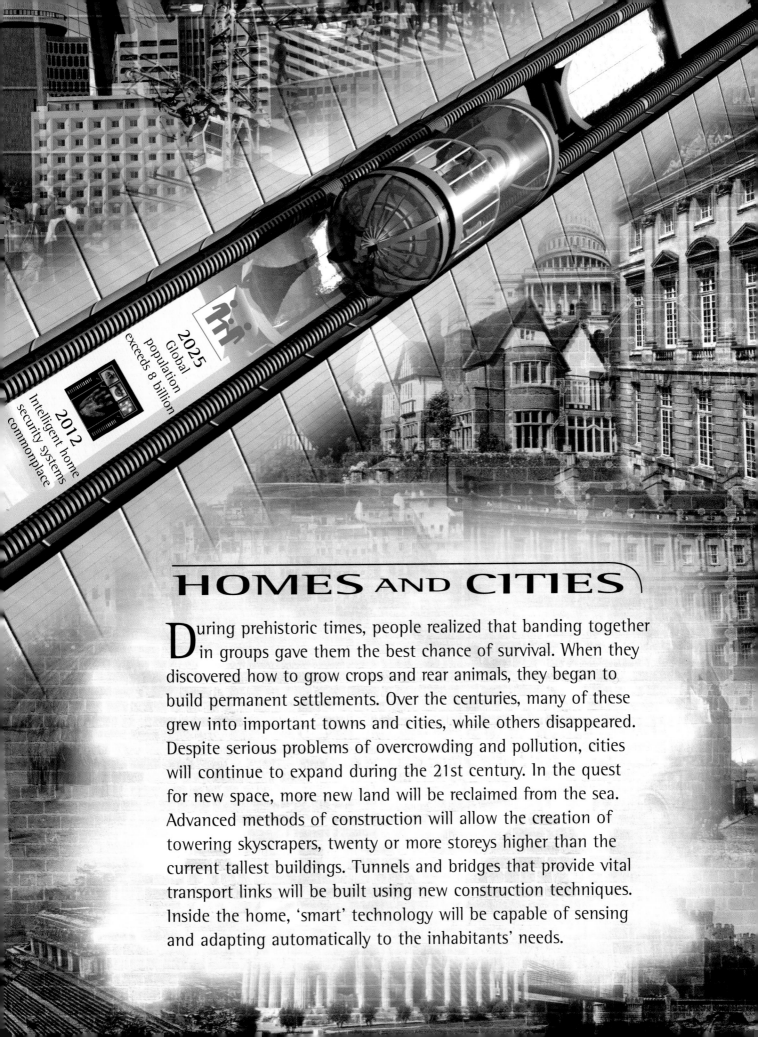

2025
Global
population
exceeds 8 billion

2012
Intelligent home
security systems
commonplace

HOMES and CITIES

During prehistoric times, people realized that banding together in groups gave them the best chance of survival. When they discovered how to grow crops and rear animals, they began to build permanent settlements. Over the centuries, many of these grew into important towns and cities, while others disappeared. Despite serious problems of overcrowding and pollution, cities will continue to expand during the 21st century. In the quest for new space, more new land will be reclaimed from the sea. Advanced methods of construction will allow the creation of towering skyscrapers, twenty or more storeys higher than the current tallest buildings. Tunnels and bridges that provide vital transport links will be built using new construction techniques. Inside the home, 'smart' technology will be capable of sensing and adapting automatically to the inhabitants' needs.

FUTURE CITY

Since the development of the first large settlements over 5,000 years ago, people have been drawn to live and work in cities and towns. Two hundred years ago, only two and half percent of the world's population lived in urban areas. By 2005, over half the world's population will live in cities, and this figure is expected to increase until the mid-21st century at least. The attraction of the city as a seat of power and a place of opportunity for learning, work and leisure will continue long into the future.

△ Athens, the capital of Greece, was the most powerful city in the world 2,500 years ago. Its public buildings have inspired architects and builders ever since.

△ Some cities evolve over many centuries. Others, such as Los Angeles in the USA, have expanded over a much shorter period. In 1890, Los Angeles had a population of 50,000. Today over nine million people live there.

△ As cities grow they tend to spread outwards as can be seen in this satellite picture of London, England. Towns and villages, once outside the city, are swallowed up and become part of the urban sprawl.

Stealing space

Space for living, working, transport and recreation is at a premium in cities and will remain a key urban issue in the future. While the 20th century saw cities grow skywards as well as continue to sprawl outwards into the countryside, future cities are also likely to create space below the ground for living and working.

Out at sea

Reclaiming land from swamps, marshes and the sea will continue to flourish in wealthy but small nations as a way of increasing available space. There is also the possibility of separate floating cities, or hybrid, part floating, part land-bound settlements, linked to the mainland. One proposed scheme is designed to provide living and working space for a million inhabitants in a vast pyramid-shaped structure in the sea off Tokyo, Japan.

▽ As future cities expand they will make use of all available space, including water, wherever possible. Environmentally friendly forms of transport such as airships will ferry people around this 2030 metropolis.

◁ Air pollution is a major problem facing many cities. Smog created by factories, power stations and road traffic can cause health problems.

Cyber city

Cyberjaya, a city currently being built in Malaysia, could provide a model for 21st-century cities. In Cyberjaya, petrol-fuelled vehicles will be banned and a low population density will be encouraged. Every home in this city will be powered by solar energy and connected to the City Command Centre – a computer network that provides information and automated services.

◁ During the English Industrial Revolution in the 1700s and 1800s, many people lived in rundown housing, or slums, when they moved from the countryside to the city.

LIVING TOGETHER

With great improvements in healthcare and breakthroughs in the fight against disease, the population of Planet Earth is booming. It is estimated that by 2025 there will be eight billion people; ten years later this will have risen to almost nine billion. This fast-growing population will place enormous strains on cities, many of which already suffer from overcrowding and a range of associated problems. Concerns about traffic, pollution and the psychological problems that result from people being forced to live very close together will continue for many years to come.

Social problems

Crowding people together in housing units or skyscrapers has not proved the best solution to the problem of finding homes for people. In the past, this kind of high-density living has led to major social problems such as drug abuse and violent crime. The search for more humane ways of housing greater numbers of people will become a dominant issue in many future cities.

▷ Not all traffic jams are caused by cars. Bicycle rickshaws have created this gridlock in Dhaka, Bangladesh. Unlike cars, however, they are non-polluting.

◁ This capsule hotel in Tokyo makes maximum use of the limited living space in the city. Hotel guests sleep in tiny units that are stacked on top of each other.

Designs for living

In existing cities, derelict areas will continue to be re-developed to house the growing population. In some cases, high-density living and working space will be crammed into a small area. Mass-transit systems and moving walkways will ferry people around quickly. Other areas will decide to take a low-density, community-led approach. These will feature smaller buildings, parks and car-free zones.

▷ Hong Kong, in China, is one of the world's most crowded places. With very little affordable housing, slums are often the only alternative.

◁ Enclosed walkways at different levels will form an extensive network connecting many parts of the city. People will be able to move around without having to negotiate the congested streets.

Getting away from it

From 2010, increasing numbers of people will turn their backs on city living. Many will move to small towns or villages to escape pollution, congestion and other urban problems. Advanced communications will enable them to telework – work from home. Others may go further and opt out of the 'rat race' altogether, living in self-sustaining communities in isolated areas.

BLURRED VISION

This imaginary flying city from a 1920s science fiction magazine is one unlikely solution to overcrowding on the planet. Writers and artists have imagined airborne cities since the 1700s.

FUTURE HOMES

The purpose-built home of the future will be designed to cocoon its inhabitants in a secure, comfortable and highly adaptable environment. Architects, engineers and designers will draw on important advances in materials technology and in electronics to create flexible living spaces that can be altered easily by the occupants. Intelligent devices will play an important role in many households. Robot cleaners and smart exercise machines that monitor health will be as common as today's microwaves and washing machines.

△ Few homes before the 1800s had any luxuries or comforts. Until labour-saving devices such as vacuum cleaners and washing machines appeared during the 1900s, all housework had to be done by hand and usually took a very long time.

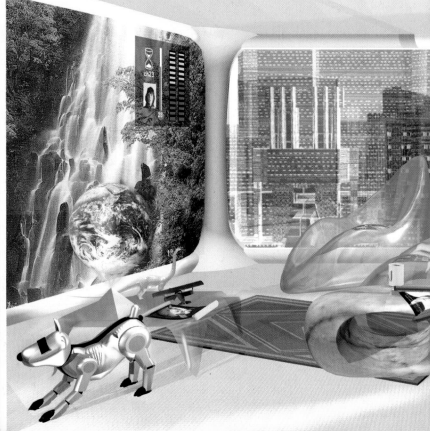

◁ Architects and engineers are re-thinking how a house functions both inside and outside. This house in California is earthquake resistant and incorporates the latest in energy-saving technology.

Intelligent home

Experts predict that by 2025 the average home will have as much computing power as a nuclear power station from the 1990s. Computers will be so small and cheap that they will be embedded, or integrated, in almost all our surroundings, from floors to fridges. They will sense our presence and automatically adjust the environment, including light, temperature and humidity levels, according to our needs.

Flexible living

Formal divisions between rooms are likely to disappear. They will be replaced by a single living space that can be sectioned off with lightweight but soundproof, moveable walls. Multi-purpose furniture will occupy living areas. Furniture structure and covering will change colour, shape and even texture at the user's request. New materials will allow a soft bench seat to transform itself into a table or desk, for example.

▷ Alternative forms of energy such as wind and solar power will provide all the energy requirements for an increasing number of homes in the future.

▽ Keys will be replaced by biometric systems that scan a person's features before giving access (*below right*).

▽ The home of 2015 will include furniture that can change its shape and colour and walls that function as giant display screens for information, leisure or just to create a relaxing environment. A robot vacuum cleaner will automatically detect and clean up spills.

Safe and secure

Traditional locks and keys will be replaced by security systems that scan a person's hand, eye or face using biometrics to determine entry. Arrays of closed-circuit TV (CCTV) cameras will be linked to a network of home security sensors far more sophisticated than today's burglar alarms. If an unauthorized person tries to enter, the house will lock up like a clam and automatically notify the police. It may even use gas sprays or hoses which would 'fire' harmless sticky foam to prevent the intruder from escaping.

△ Some architects and builders are rejecting the latest technology in favour of simple homes constructed from natural, locally found materials.

Robots at work

By 2020, robots with sophisticated sensor and control systems will be phased into construction work. They will perform a range of tasks including welding, painting and fixing cladding or tiles to the external surfaces of buildings. Free-flying robot cameras will move around the site and provide views of the work in progress from all angles.

◁ A pre-fabricated wall section is hoisted into position by a crane on this skyscraper construction site of the 2020s. It is fitted with arrays of photo-voltaic cells which generate electricity from sunlight. Robots weld girders together while flying robot cameras monitor the site.

◁ Construction of the Empire State Building began in March 1930 and was completed in May 1931. It has 102 storeys and contains over 285 kilometres of steel beams.

Hazard proof

Earthquakes pose a major threat to some of the world's major cities including San Francisco, USA, and Tokyo, Japan. New construction techniques are helping to make some structures more earthquake resistant. The Tokyo Forum building, for example, has glass walls supported independently from its roof. During an earthquake, the roof rocks on powerful joints, preventing the building from crashing down.

CONSTRUCTION

Materials are at the very heart of the construction industry. In the foreseeable future, buildings will continue to be built using steel, concrete, bricks and glass but there will also be far greater use of composites and new metal alloys. These new materials, along with advanced computer modelling, will allow architects and engineers to design even bigger buildings, tunnels and bridges and to locate them in places that are currently unsuitable. A further innovation will be tiny sensors inside the materials that automatically measure and report any deterioration.

△ Geodesic domes are strong, lightweight structures that do not require internal supports. They can enclose large areas using far less material than standard frames.

Bridging the gap

Some of the most important construction projects are bridges. The development of exceptionally strong materials as well as computer modelling is allowing engineers to design increasingly ambitious structures. Proposed projects include the 3.3 km-long Messina Straits Bridge to link mainland Italy to Sicily, and a massive 5 km-long bridge across the Straits of Gibraltar, to join Europe to North Africa.

▷ The 451-metre high Petronas Towers in Malaysia have over 32,000 windows.

◁ Powerful computers allow engineers to test structures for stresses and strains long before they are constructed.

CRYSTAL BALL

An increasing number of homes will be built underground during the 21st century. Underground homes offer a spacious alternative to cramped conditions on the surface, and are naturally cool, even in very hot climates.

TRANSPORT

Until the middle of the 19th century, the majority of people rarely travelled more than a few kilometres from their homes. When people set out on a journey the choice was limited – by boat or ship, by horse or by foot. With the invention of the steam locomotive in the 1800s, and later the development of road vehicles and aircraft, modern transport opened up a whole new world for many people. During the 21st century, many forms of transport will become faster, safer and less damaging to the environment. Electric-powered cars, which cause minimal pollution, will be commonplace on the roads by 2025. Shipping and rail will also benefit from exciting new forms of power such as magnetic propulsion. For longer journeys, hypersonic and sub-orbital airliners may cut flying time by up to two-thirds.

1640
First taxi service begins in Paris

1790
The velocipede, forerunner of the modern bicycle, is invented

1830
Inter-city railway service is introduced between Manchester and Liverpool, England

1903
First flight made by a heavier-than-air craft, the Wright brother's Flyer

1908
First mass produced car, the Model T Ford

2035
It takes under two hours to fly half-way across the world

2010
New generation of safe airships carry passengers and heavy goods

1981
French TGV high-speed train service introduced

1959
First commercial service by hovercraft in operation

▽ Concept 2096 is one research team's vision of the car for the end of the century. Passengers will be encased in an extremely tough protective shell. The car will be driven automatically using guide transmitters fitted to the roads.

△ Early cars looked like horseless carriages. The Lutzmann car, built in 1895, was powered by a simple internal combustion engine.

FUTURE CAR

When the first cars took to the roads in the 1880s and 1890s, their top speed rarely exceeded 20 km/h. The brakes were usually ineffective and engines often exploded. A century ago, no one could have predicted the global increase in road vehicles which today number hundreds of millions. Modern cars may be much faster, more comfortable and fuel-efficient than their predecessors but like the first cars, most rely on pollution–causing oil derivatives. The future is likely to see popular alternatives to purely petrol-driven vehicles – machines that offer comparable performance but at far lower cost to the planet.

△ Most electric cars today have a limited range and can only travel about 100 kilometres before their batteries need to be re-charged. This re-charging point is built into a parking space in Los Angeles, USA.

Fighting pollution

Although modern internal combustion-engine cars are 'cleaner' than in the past, their exhaust emissions still cause damage to the atmosphere. Many ideas have been put forward to lessen the impact. These include more fuel-efficient and lightweight cars and an increase in electric vehicle production. Other initiatives include the promotion of public transport and the banning of cars from the centre of towns.

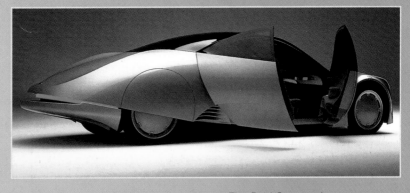

△ The Ford Synergy is a prototype vehicle driven by hybrid propulsion. It could be in production by 2010.

△ By making cars lighter, they can be made more fuel-efficient and, in the case of the McClaren F1, much faster. This supercar has a lightweight carbon fibre body shell.

A host of extras

Despite joystick-controlled prototypes, the steering wheel is likely to remain a feature in most cars for many years to come. However, steering and other driver tasks such as navigation, braking and gear changing will benefit from advances in on-board computer systems. Drivers will also use voice-activated mapping and route trackers and their e-mail will be read to them via a speech synthesizer.

Best of both worlds

Hybrid propulsion offers a compromise between clean, electric-powered cars and higher performance petrol-driven models. The electric motor, which gives off no emissions, is operated in built-up areas and at low speeds. On the open road, away from urban areas, the petrol-driven engine takes over. Hybrid cars cause up to ten times less pollution than conventional cars and are expected to be a popular class of vehicle by 2010.

BLURRED VISION

Predictions that self-driving vehicles would take to the roads by 2000 have proved wide of the mark. However, in the near future, powerful sensors and more effective control systems will aid drivers and make journeys by road much safer.

ON THE ROAD

By 2015, a growing number of towns and cities will promote bikes, electric-powered single person vehicles and new public transport initiatives. However, the most far-reaching change to road networks will be Intelligent Traffic Systems (ITS). By 2020, ITS could be in full operation in the USA, Japan and Europe. ITS use computer networks to manage traffic, keep vehicles a set distance apart and advise drivers on the best route. It promises congestion-free roads, as well as a major reduction in accidents and huge savings in fuel consumption because of more efficient route planning.

△ During the 20th century, many cities suffered from serious road congestion. This scene from 1912 shows slow-moving traffic in the centre of London.

Traffic management

Advanced Intelligent Traffic Systems will be based on a sophisticated network of sensors. These will map an entire road system and communicate with on-board vehicle computers. By 2025, platooning may be in operation. In this system, cars travel in a convoy – each car's speed and distance from other vehicles is automatically controlled.

▽ By 2020, many road networks will have Intelligent Traffic Systems (ITS). Sensors will be built alongside and in the road. These will be linked to a central computer that relays traffic data to drivers. As well as making road travel safer and faster, ITS will identify dangerous driving and speeding.

◁ The Mercedes *Life-Jet* is a hybrid motorcycle-car. This form of transport is very fuel efficient and is likely to become a popular vehicle during the 21st century.

Pedal power

Single-person vehicles, much smaller than today's cars and powered by electric motors, may be a popular choice of transport by 2015. There is also likely to be growing pressure to create more bike-friendly cities. This would involve building secure bike storage areas and separate fast-track cycleways.

Self-diagnosis

By 2010, many cars will be built with a fully integrated central computer connected to sensors throughout the vehicle. The computer will monitor most aspects of the car's running from brake quality to engine timing. The computer will automatically maximize performance and efficiency, warn of potential malfunctions and communicate directly with a breakdown service. Using a system called telemetry, the breakdown service may even be able to fix certain internal faults over the airwaves.

△ The Urban Dream bicycle is one of a new breed of folding bikes that uses lightweight materials for true portability. These bikes can easily be carried in one hand, and are ideal for commuters to move quickly around city centres.

▷ The recumbent bicycle will become a common sight on roads in the future. Cycling in this position places far less stress on the body and allows the cyclist to travel faster for longer.

◁ Advanced in-car electronic entertainment will be an optional feature in most production vehicles by 2010. Screens fitted to the backs of seats will provide games, movies and Internet access.

◁ Before the invention of the steam-powered locomotive in the 1800s, wagons and carts pulled by animals were the fastest methods of moving goods by land.

FERRYING PEOPLE AND GOODS

Civilizations – both past and present – have always depended on the effective transportation of supplies, materials, goods and people. The invention of engine-powered vehicles, in the early 1800s, dramatically increased the speed of transportation and the amount of freight which could be moved. A growth in population means not only a greater demand for goods and materials, but also greater pressure on public transport. It is estimated that by 2023, passengers across the world will travel more than 88 trillion kilometres, which is twice today's figure. Alternative modes of transport, such as magnetic levitation trains and airships are expected to ease some of the pressure.

Airship revival

Airships were a popular form of transport until a series of accidents in the 1920s and 1930s. Current versions use non-flammable gas and are expected to make a major comeback, especially as freight carriers. Although airships are slow, they provide massive lifting potential. By 2020, 400-metre airships will be capable of carrying up to 300 tonnes of cargo over distances of more than 8,000 km.

△ Standardized containers have transformed the way cargo is moved around the world. Railcars, lifting apparatus, trucks and ships form a fully integrated transportation system.

△ The Transrapid monorail link is expected to open in Germany in 2005. It will connect the cities of Hamburg and Berlin, carrying passengers at speeds of 500 km/h.

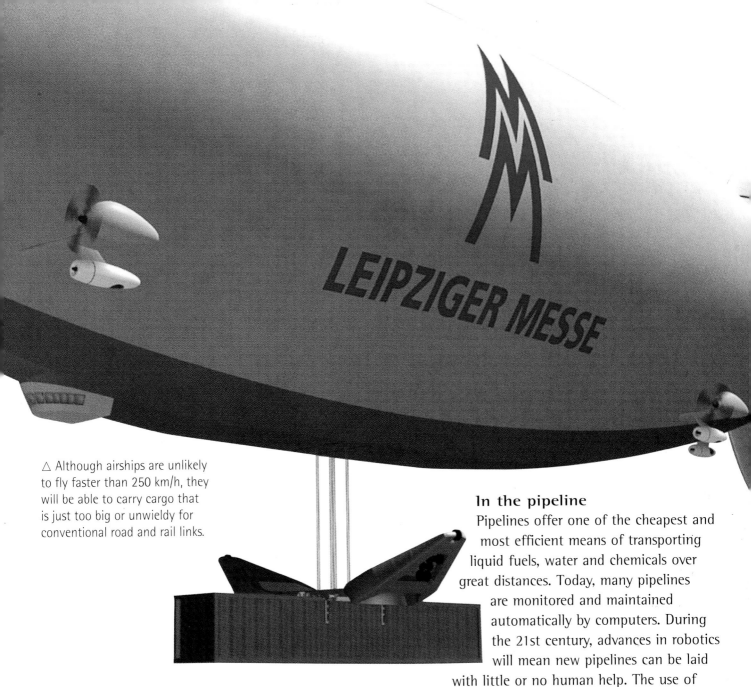

△ Although airships are unlikely to fly faster than 250 km/h, they will be able to carry cargo that is just too big or unwieldy for conventional road and rail links.

In the pipeline
Pipelines offer one of the cheapest and most efficient means of transporting liquid fuels, water and chemicals over great distances. Today, many pipelines are monitored and maintained automatically by computers. During the 21st century, advances in robotics will mean new pipelines can be laid with little or no human help. The use of waterflow to carry solid materials such as iron ore and coal is also likely to increase.

Support your railway
Many governments already encourage greater use of public transport and rail freight systems to ease overcrowded roads. We can expect to see increased investment in mass-transit systems, including driverless trains running underground or suspended from overhead tracks. High-speed trains, running at 450 km/h or more, may either be electric or powered by magnetic levitation. Analysts predict that they will carry as many as a third of all overland passengers by 2040.

CRYSTAL BALL
By 2050, pipelines pumped full of air under pressure may transport capsules containing goods above and below ground as well as through water. These capsule systems may also carry people.

SEA TRANSPORT

▷ Until the arrival of steamships in the early 1800s, long distance journeys by sea had to be undertaken by sailing ships. These relied on the unpredictability of the wind for propulsion.

Sail revival

A new form of traditional technology is likely to appear on many ships. By 2015, tankers and giant container ships may be fitted with solid sails to complement the regular engines. The sails will be computer-controlled to take advantage of the wind, whatever its direction. This system, although dependent on weather conditions, will offer fuel savings of up to 25 percent.

It has been almost a century since sea transport provided the fastest and, in some cases, the only link between distant places. However, shipping continues to be one of the most effective methods of moving goods and materials around the planet. New propulsion systems will help cut transport times and this will encourage more industries to transport freight by sea. Passenger vessels will also grow in popularity. For shorter journeys, small ferries will carry people across the water at high speed. At the other end of the scale, a new generation of ocean liners carrying up to 5,000 people will become floating cities, with shopping malls, ice rinks and even artificial beaches on board.

▷ This ground effect craft of 2030 skims the surface on a cushion of air created by its giant wings. Ground effect craft will also be able to cross flat, isolated areas and icy wastes.

Magnet power

Magnetohydrodynamic (MHD) propulsion could become a common form of sea propulsion by the 2030s. MHD uses a superconducting magnet to generate a powerful electric field around tubes filled with seawater. An electric current passed through the water generates a strong force that drives the water out of the tubes and the craft forward. MHD has no moving parts, takes up little room, works well at high speeds and creates little noise or vibration. MHD propulsion may power new generations of superfast, short-distance ferries as well as long-distance cruisers and military 'stealth' ships.

△ The *Solar Sailor* uses large modules of waterproofed solar cells to provide power. The sails can be tilted at any angle to catch the sunlight as well as any wind.

◁ The *Yamato 1* is the world's first boat to be powered by magnetohydrodynamic propulsion. Thrust is provided by an electric current passed through seawater. Future vessels will be capable of speeds of up to 90 km/h.

△ Sailing boats are still a popular choice for leisure and sporting activities. Advanced sail systems and computer-controlled weather and navigation systems make these lightweight yachts safer and extremely manoeuvrable.

Flying boats

By 2020, a new kind of vessel that looks – and acts – more like a plane than a ship may be in operation. Ground effect craft will use the extra lift generated by a wing flying a few metres above the surface of the water to cruise at speeds of up to 450 km/h. The reduced drag created by this form of propulsion will make these craft extremely fuel efficient. Ground effect craft will be able to carry very large payloads – or up to 600 passengers – but at much lower cost than conventional air transport.

▷ The *Carnival Destiny*, built in 1996, can carry over 2,500 passengers in great luxury. It is the length of three football pitches and at 56 metres is taller than the Statue of Liberty.

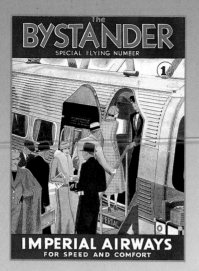

The BYSTANDER
SPECIAL FLYING NUMBER

IMPERIAL AIRWAYS
FOR SPEED AND COMFORT

◁ During the 1930s, air travel was a luxury that only the wealthy could afford. Aircraft seated small numbers of people and usually had to land and refuel every 300 to 400 kilometres.

AIRPORTS AND AIR TRAVEL

The number of air passengers is expected to triple over the first twenty years of the 21st century, placing enormous demands on airports around the world. Many airports are already at their full capacity. Building more runways is not the answer as city locations and crowded airspace mean there is little room for further expansion. One solution is to build bigger airliners and new airports. Floating airports are another possibility, as is the use of land reclaimed from the sea. However, the most radical changes to airports are likely to take place inside the passenger terminals.

▷ In the future, faster processing of passengers and more reliable aircraft will help prevent unnecessary delays, and overcrowded scenes such as this one at Gatwick Airport in England.

Smoother procedures

Automated passenger handling systems will remove many of the lengthy administration procedures that affect air travellers today. By 2010, advanced imaging systems and powerful computers will mean that procedures such as passport control and security checks can be performed automatically, without the delays caused by human intervention. Time spent on the ground will be significantly reduced and this in turn will help reduce overcrowding in terminals.

△ Electronic tagging will ensure your luggage never gets lost. Screens built into the casing will display all relevant flight information.

◁ Electronic passport control, as well as body and baggage checks, will be performed by a single walk-through scanner system. This will allow for much faster departures and arrivals.

▽ Some airlines have already introduced automated ticket dispensers that reduce check-in, ticketing and boarding times.

Local air transport

Short-haul air transport from city to city or even within a metropolitan area is likely to receive a major boost by 2010 with the arrival of fleets of tilt-rotor aircraft. These aircraft are capable of short or vertical take-off and landing because they can tilt their turboshaft engines upwards. For regular flight, the engines are returned to a horizontal position. With cruise speeds of around 450–550 km/h, tilt-rotor aircraft are much faster, quieter and more fuel-efficient than helicopters.

Cabin flexibility

In the early years of the 21st century, air travellers can expect to see two new trends. For short-haul flights, some aircraft will be designed without cargo holds but with larger cabin storage instead. These fast-track flights will offer much quicker, regular services for walk-on, walk-off passengers. For long-distance flights, travellers who can afford it will have their own private sleeping cabins. These will be constructed with foldaway beds and ceiling storage to maximize space.

△ Hong Kong Airport opened in 1998. Its main terminal is 1.3 km long, has driverless trains and 54 moving walkways. The airport can handle up to 87 million passengers a year.

AIRLINERS

Aircraft have come a long way since the first wood and canvas contraptions took to the air at the beginning of the 20th century. Air travel has transformed millions of people's lives by making it possible to travel abroad or make long journeys that in the past would have taken days or even months. Aircraft will become even faster and continue to grow in size, some carrying up to a thousand passengers at a time. Long-range aircraft that do not need to re-fuel will cut travelling time on long-haul flights by up to a third. But the most exciting proposals are for high-speed airliners that use rocket engines to blast the craft into space.

△ The De Havilland *Comet* was the world's first jet airliner. It entered service in 1952 and could carry 36 passengers.

Increased capacity

In 1997, there were over 1.6 billion air travellers. This figure is expected to rise to over 5 billion by 2020. To cope with the additional demand, larger aircraft will be built for the more popular routes. Two-tiered airliners carrying up to 700 passengers will be in service by 2020 and 900-seater models by 2030. Airports and boarding procedures will also have to be radically altered to cope with the rapid increase in passenger numbers.

△ The Airbus Industries A3XX is expected to be in service by 2006. This new breed of mega-jumbo will seat 555 passengers and have a range of over 14,000 kilometres. Future versions will carry over 650 people.

The pursuit of speed

The first supersonic aircraft began flying regular passenger services in the 1970s. *Concorde* can fly at speeds of 2,400 km/h – almost three times the speed of conventional aircraft. The next generation of high-speed craft will be be hypersonic, flying at Mach 5 and above (*Concorde* cruises just above Mach 2). Some hypersonic designs will be sub-orbital – powerful rocket engines will boost the aircraft into partial orbit around the Earth. The aircraft will then glide down to its destination.

▽▷ Hypersoar will fire its air-breathing engines to fly to the edge of the Earth's atmosphere and into space. It will then shut down its engines and glide down to an altitude of 40km before firing its engines again. This trajectory prevents overheating in the extremely hot atmosphere. Hypersoar will carry passengers to the other side of the world in under two hours.

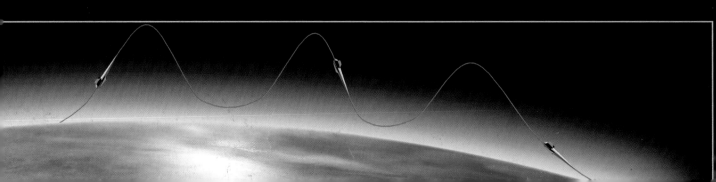

Out of this world

One of the most revolutionary proposals for future aircraft design is the Hypersoar craft. Hypersoar will skim the top of the Earth's atmosphere in a unique skipping trajectory, operating its engines in short bursts. It will fly and coast back to Earth at speeds of up to 10,000 km/h. By 2035, Hypersoar aircraft could be in operation flying express mail and special services. Larger, passenger-carrying craft may be launched five or ten years later.

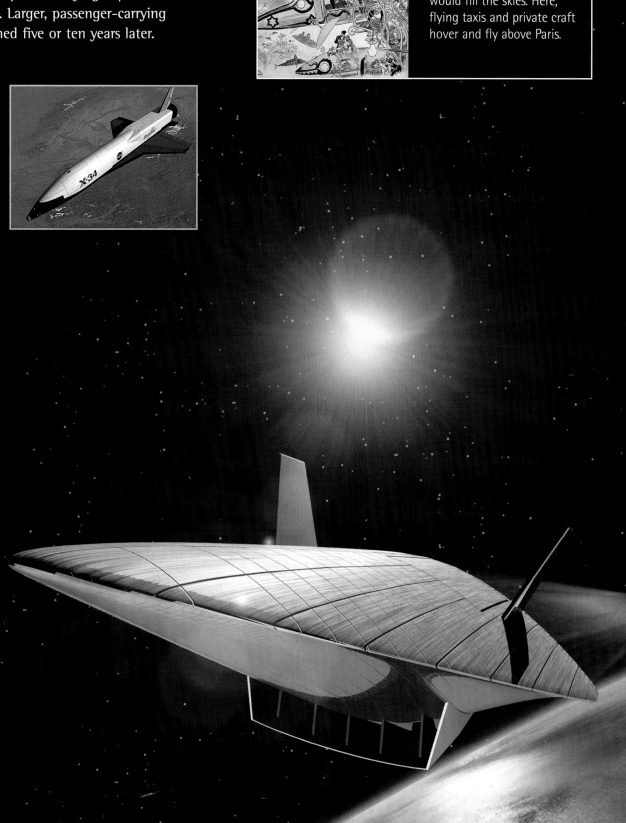

BLURRED VISION

At the beginning of the 20th century some people envisaged that a constant traffic of flying machines would fill the skies. Here, flying taxis and private craft hover and fly above Paris.

▷ The X-34 reusable rocket is likely to be the successor to the space shuttle. Some of its technology is likely to be used in sub-orbital and hypersonic airliners.

1760s
Industrial Revolution in Britain changes the way people work

1800s
Development of organized rules for many sports

1870s
First practical typewriters used in offices

1938
Photocopier machines appear

1950
First credit cards in use

1960s
Cost of air travel plummets – air travel now available to many people

1980s
Arrival of affordable personal computers

WORK AND PLAY

In the last two decades of the 20th century, computers and new technology dramatically changed the the way we work and live. The Information Revolution will continue to transform society in almost every area from education to leisure pursuits. Full-time jobs will become increasingly scarce with a growing number of people in part-time work. Many offices will close as people work from home, linked by videophones, teleconferencing and intelligent computer networks, a thousand times faster than the current Internet. The search for work will involve scouring the whole globe, not just the local area. When not working you will be able to visit local artificial resorts, climate-controlled by technology to mimic more distant and exotic locations. However, as everyday environments become increasingly secure and controlled, some people will seek their thrills by pursuing new adrenaline-inducing sports.

2060
Machines directly
controlled by mind

2040
First holidays in
orbiting space hotels

2010s
Huge increase in
people teleworking

THE WAY TO WORK

Today we are living in the early years of the Information Revolution. The number of people in manufacturing industries will continue to decline – by 2025, under two percent of the workforce in the developed world will work in factories. Jobs involving computers and communications will continue to increase. Other major growth areas will include tourism and professional care for an increasingly ageing population. Many jobs were once for life. In the future, most employment will be short-term, away from a fixed base, and it will rely on technology to link workers and customers.

△ In the early part of the 20th century, working conditions in offices were often cramped and uncomfortable.

△▷ By 2010, wearable computers will provide complete office facilities for workers on the move. An alternative to the office-on-the-arm system uses a headset to create the illusion of a full-size computer screen.

Teleworking

Many people already work from home or away from the company that employs them. Teleworking will continue to expand, affecting millions of workers, from technical support staff to salespeople. Links to customers and co-workers will be provided by high-speed data networks, multi-line telephone systems and real-time, high-quality video cameras. Computers may even measure aspects of an employee's work performance.

◁ A laptop computer linked to a modem and satellite mobile phone allows people working in the most isolated areas to keep in touch with colleagues almost anywhere in the world.

▽ Many meetings in the workplace of the future are likely to use advanced communications such as this 3-D holographic system to bring people together. Holography uses lasers to produce life-like images.

Flexible workers

Current trends in employment such as shorter term contracts, more women in work, and more part-time jobs will continue well into the 21st century. By 2010, it is estimated that more than 40 percent of workers will be women. Despite the growth of teleworking, however, not everyone will operate from home – a significant part of the workforce will become much more mobile. Fewer international barriers and restrictions will allow far more people to travel abroad in a global search for different kinds of work.

Future offices

Although more people will work at home, offices will not disappear. Many will evolve into communications centres for employees to use. The buildings will become intelligent spaces for workers on the move and will be highly flexible. Staff will find themselves hot-desking – using whichever desk is available when they come in to work. Smart desks with built-in global communications, computing and copying facilities will recognize and respond to each user.

◁ VR technology will be used increasingly in the design and testing of products before they are built. Here, engineers and technicians are studying the construction of a car.

△ Teleconferencing uses real-time cameras to provide instant visual communication with people not physically present in a room. By 2020, teleconferencing will become much more realistic with a new generation of holographic systems.

In today's Information Age, knowledge means power. The ability to access information, understand it and communicate it to other people has become highly prized. Education will play a central role in developing these skills. On-line education, virtual classrooms and electronic books (e-books) will be an essential part of schooling by the 2020s. Virtual tutors will be available to many pre-school children. Traditional elements of school life such as group activities, educational trips and printed books will not disappear altogether, but they will be eclipsed by technological alternatives.

△ In the early years of the 20th century, teaching in many schools relied on strict discipline and inflexible learning techiques.

FUTURE LEARNING

The end of print?

The arrival of affordable e-books, from 2010 onwards, may revolutionize how we read. E-books are lightweight electronic machines capable of storing a number of books and magazines downloaded from the Internet. A single e-book will be able to hold a student's entire course work. E-books waste no paper but still allow users to scribble notes on the text with electronic pens. By 2050, printed books may become collectors' items.

School days

By 2030, pupils will spend more time working from home. Structured lessons will use 3-D holographic projection systems while high-speed data links will enable teleconferencing to take place between teachers and students. But time spent interacting with fellow pupils at school will still be recognized as an important part of education.

△ Every generation can benefit from learning via the computer. The ability to send interactive course and lesson modules over the Internet will revolutionize education during the 21st century.

▷ Learning how to use a computer is fast becoming one of the most basic skills for children in the first years of education.

◁ Books still offer unique advantages over computers. They are cheap, portable and provide easy access to information. However, over the next few decades, books will be replaced by e-books.

On-going learning

In the future, education will not end when you are 16, 18 or 21. In the rapidly changing Information Age, education will be a lifelong process. People will need to acquire many new skills during their lifetimes. Adults may enrol on three or more degree courses while learning aids plugged into e-books will provide primers and instant updating sessions for many skills.

▷ Interactive displays are a fun and important way of learning at many zoos, museums and nature parks. At the London Aquarium, the public are encouraged to interact with some of the marine life.

△ Virtual Reality headsets and data gloves will feature in many schools and homes by 2020. VR can help explain complex topics, such as the atomic structure of elements, in an exciting and effective way.

△ At the end of the 19th century, Egypt had become a destination for wealthy tourists. However, mass tourism is much more recent and emerged only with the arrival of cheap air fares in the 1960s.

In the time it takes you to read this sentence, over 3,000 people, some for business but the majority for pleasure, will have taken to the air to travel to another country. Travel and tourism are now the world's biggest industries, generating almost 12 percent of global income. By 2025, the number of tourists is expected to double and at least four million new jobs in the travel and tourism industry will be created each year. There will also be a greater range of options for the holidaymaker. Traditional destinations will remain popular but people will also be offered new travel opportunities such as holidays underwater and in space.

TOURISM AND TRAVEL

▽ Scuba divers are just one of the sights you can expect to see from your bedroom window in this underwater hotel off the coast of Florida, USA.

Travel trends

One area that will probably face a serious decline is the travel agent industry. This sector will suffer because of the ease and convenience of buying flights and accommodation directly over the Internet. Another technological innovation is likely to be in-ear translation systems. By 2020, an earpiece and tiny microphone will be able to translate in real-time most foreign languages with 90 percent accuracy.

New locations

Despite environmental pressures, it is likely that hotels will be built in the Arctic and Antarctic by 2025. By the middle of the 21st century, space hotels orbiting the Earth may be a popular but expensive destination. Long before then we can expect to see a massive boom in underwater resorts in seas and oceans. All these new destinations will rely on technology to create a comfortable and safe environment for the holidaymaker.

In the second half of the 21st century, holidaymakers will be able to choose destinations that lie beyond the Earth. Water, frozen in rocks on the Moon, may be used to supply and support a hotel and base.

Access denied

Although tourism generates massive amounts of wealth, it can also create a number of problems such as damage to the environment and threats to sites of cultural importance. The potentially destructive effects caused by greater number of tourists will lead to a rise in environmental protests and many historical sites becoming closed to the public.

▷ Since the 1990s, there has been an increased demand for less conventional holidays. Antarctica and other protected wilderness areas are becoming established destinations for high-paying tourists.

◁ By 2010, underwater hotels will operate in popular holiday areas such as the Caribbean, Hawaii and the South Pacific. Tourist submersibles will ferry people to and from the hotels as well as taking them on seabed sightseeing trips.

LEISURE ACTIVITIES

△ Football fans in the 1890s were crammed together in the open. Sports stadia of the 21st century will offer a whole range of comforts and features, such as LCD screens fitted into seats.

Predictions of a world in which most people are freed from work and household drudgery so that they can live a life of complete leisure will not become a reality during the 21st century. Even so, the amount of leisure time available to many people will increase as a result of shorter working hours, less commuting, labour-saving household devices and services such as Internet shopping. Many traditional activities including sport will continue. But we can also expect Virtual Reality simulators, sophisticated interactive television and the creation of new indoor artificial environments.

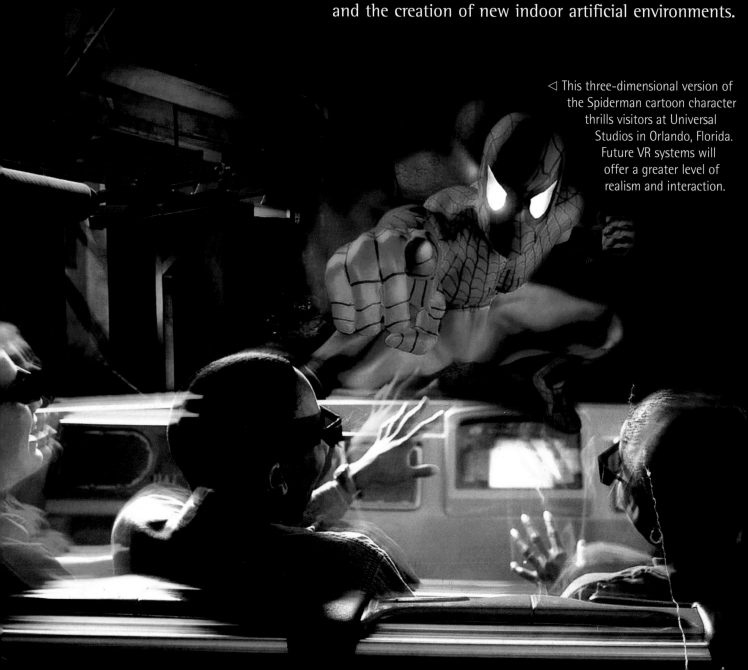

◁ This three-dimensional version of the Spiderman cartoon character thrills visitors at Universal Studios in Orlando, Florida. Future VR systems will offer a greater level of realism and interaction.

◁ Giant fans generate wind conditions of up to 25 knots in this wind-surfing arena in Paris, France. Future sport centres will produce even more life-like conditions.

▽ Sarcos is a robot capable of recognizing and reacting to a human table tennis player's moves. Robotic opponents are likely to become a popular feature of future game centres.

Inside the Dome

Not all leisure time will be spent at home. You may be able to visit a new kind of exotic location that is just a short journey from where you live. During the 21st century, we can expect to see the rise in popularity of leisure domes. Such structures already exist in Japan. They recreate a variety of different environments such as tropical beaches or winter resorts. The weather outdoors is never a problem as the domes are completely self-contained and maintain a constant climate.

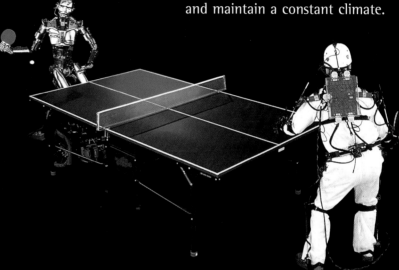

Stay at home

Future homes, equipped with the latest technology, will be the place where millions of people choose to spend most of their leisure time. Advanced exercise machines that simulate outdoor activities will be a common feature as people spend more time indoors. Entertainment systems will become increasingly interactive. For example, you will be able to watch sporting events from a vast array of different camera angles or run your own instant replays.

Another world

Virtual Reality (VR), which generates a realistic three-dimensional world around a person, has the potential to revolutionize games and entertainment. By 2015, today's cumbersome VR helmets are likely to be replaced by lightweight displays or glasses that project images directly into the eye. By 2025, VR bodysuits will create a new level of realism by using a system of sensors and tiny mechanical devices that simulate all the senses.

▷ The Seagaia Ocean resort complex in Miyazaki, Japan, is the world's most advanced all-weather indoor resort. It can hold 10,000 visitors.

◁ Rollercoasters have provided adrenaline-pumping excitement for millions of visitors to fair and theme parks since the first models were built in the late 1800s.

ADRENALINE SPORTS

For future generations, life in cities will become increasingly secure and structured. Many leisure activities will reflect this and use technology to create harmless, artificial environments. But for some people this will not be enough. There will be a major growth in activities that mimic the fear and the thrill people experience when they are in real danger. These activities are sometimes known as adrenaline sports after the chemical that the human body secretes when it is extremely excited. For those who do not want to take such risks, microprocessor implants may simulate these experiences by the middle of the century.

◁ A bungee jumper, attached only by a strong, elastic rope, freefalls through the air. The rope pulls the jumper back before impact with the ground.

Searching for the ultimate high
Traditional high-risk sports such as climbing, caving, free-fall and parachuting will continue to attract people who are looking for an element of danger in their leisure activities. Newer, more extreme sports and activities will also evolve – including illegal ones such as hangliding from the tops of tall buildings.

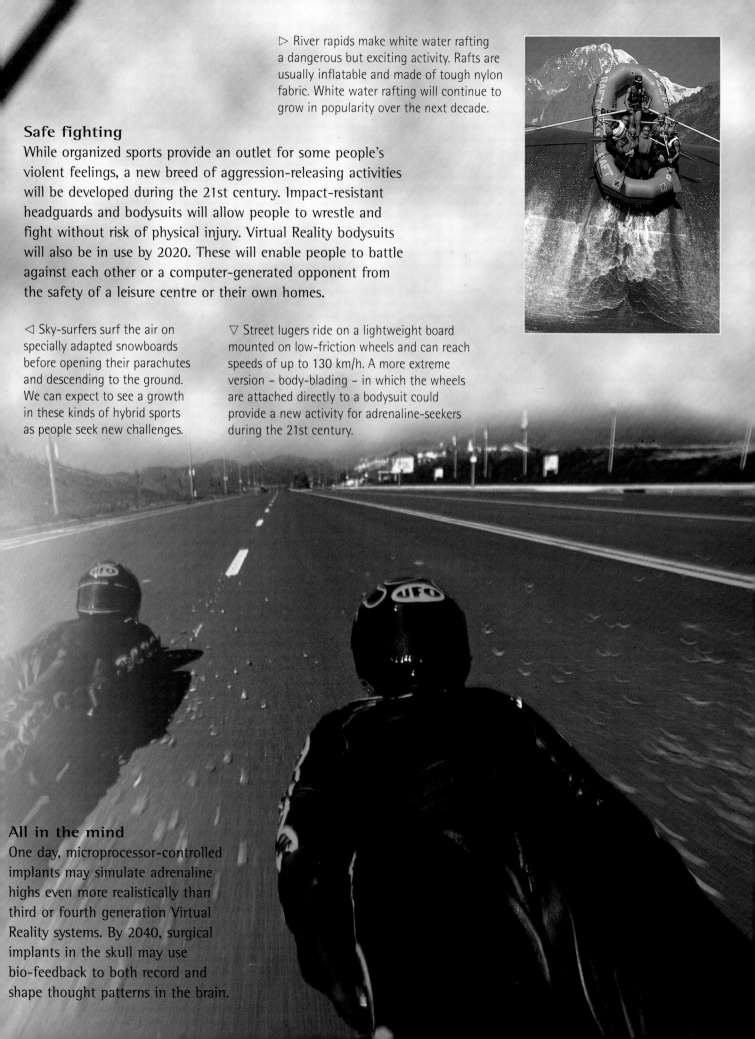

▷ River rapids make white water rafting a dangerous but exciting activity. Rafts are usually inflatable and made of tough nylon fabric. White water rafting will continue to grow in popularity over the next decade.

Safe fighting

While organized sports provide an outlet for some people's violent feelings, a new breed of aggression-releasing activities will be developed during the 21st century. Impact-resistant headguards and bodysuits will allow people to wrestle and fight without risk of physical injury. Virtual Reality bodysuits will also be in use by 2020. These will enable people to battle against each other or a computer-generated opponent from the safety of a leisure centre or their own homes.

◁ Sky-surfers surf the air on specially adapted snowboards before opening their parachutes and descending to the ground. We can expect to see a growth in these kinds of hybrid sports as people seek new challenges.

▽ Street lugers ride on a lightweight board mounted on low-friction wheels and can reach speeds of up to 130 km/h. A more extreme version – body-blading – in which the wheels are attached directly to a bodysuit could provide a new activity for adrenaline-seekers during the 21st century.

All in the mind

One day, microprocessor-controlled implants may simulate adrenaline highs even more realistically than third or fourth generation Virtual Reality systems. By 2040, surgical implants in the skull may use bio-feedback to both record and shape thought patterns in the brain.

2050
Effective
cloud-seeding
to create rain
in use

2020
Human body
parts grown in
animals become
available

2010
Many common
medicines grown
in plants using
biotechnology

2005
Human Genome
Project completed

HEALTHY LIVING

During the 21st century, people will live longer and lead healthier lives than ever before. Improved healthcare, further breakthroughs in understanding how the body works, and even the possibility of growing spare body parts will improve the lives of millions of people. Advances in genetics will allow doctors to screen and treat people – sometimes while still in the womb – for many diseases that are currently incurable. Major developments are also expected in biotechnology and farming. Far greater yields in food production along with more effective water management has the potential to prevent the terrible famines and droughts that afflicted many developing nations during the 20th century. The cost of good health, caring for an increasingly ageing population, and providing water and food for all will dominate the politics of many countries over the next century.

1978
First test-tube baby born in England

1958
Heart pacemaker invented

1955
First successful polio vaccine

1928
Discovery of penicillin

1851
Mechanical reaper revolutionizes farming

1796
First vaccinations developed by Edward Jenner

△ Fresh water was not readily available for most people before the 1900s. Today, in some countries, many people still do not have access to water in their homes.

In developed nations, clean water, waste disposal and sanitation are often taken for granted – until there are water shortages or blockages in pipes and drains. This is not the case, however, for millions of people in developing nations where sanitation or access to clean water can mean the difference between life and death. During the 21st century, new techniques in supplying and generating water, along with improvements in weather forecasting, will have a global benefit.

WEATHER, WATER AND WASTE

△ Global warming may become partly responsible for major droughts during the 21st century. These will put a great strain on the world's water supplies.

The big issues

Although fresh water is abundant on a global scale, it is often very scarce locally. It has been estimated that over a billion people around the world lack access to safe water. More effective and fairer distribution of water will become a priority during the 21st century. Governments must also ensure that existing water supplies such as rivers do not become unusable as a result of pollution.

Disposal

Approximately 30 litres of fresh water are used each time someone flushes a toilet. Waste needs to be removed but we need to find alternatives that involve as little water as possible in the process. Waterless toilets that use layers of bacteria in sealed tanks to digest waste and turn it into harmless compost are one possibility. They require no water and prevent the spread of disease.

◁ Desalination plants use up large amounts of energy but are capable of turning salt water into fresh water. Future plants may be considerably more energy-efficient.

◁ Vast quantities of industrial waste, called effluent, are poured into rivers, polluting water supplies. Unless this is stopped, many valuable sources of fresh water will become unsuitable, even after treatment at waterworks.

Fresh water for all

In some areas where water is scarce, efforts may turn to water generation rather than collection and distribution. Cost-effective extraction of fresh water from salt water at desalination plants is likely in the near future. By 2050, altering the chemical structure of clouds, or cloud-seeding, may be used to make rain where it is most needed.

△ The Meteosat weather satellite, built by the European Space Agency, transmits an image of cloud patterns back to a ground base on Earth every 30 minutes.

◁ By the middle of the 21st century, vast fleets of insect-size cloud-seeding machines, or mesicopters, may be launched in areas with little rainfall. Once inside the clouds, the mesicopters will release chemical particles that cause water vapour to form and fall as rain.

▷ The development of new materials and advances in micro-engineering will allow the manufacture of very cheap and extremely small machines.

▷ The mechanical reaping machine, invented by Cyrus Hall McCormick in 1851, allowed farmers to quadruple the amount of grain they could harvest.

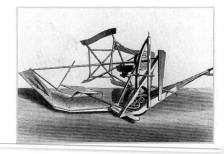

FUTURE FARMING

For thousands of years, most of the world's population farmed the land. Crops were grown and animals were raised in order to support each family. Any surplus was taken to market for sale. The Agricultural Revolution in Europe during the 1700s began a process which we still see today – a small proportion of people producing food for the majority. During the 21st century, technology such as 'smart' harvesting machinery, biotechnology and hydroponics will continue to make farming more efficient. Even so, it will take a great deal of political will, as well as scientific advances, to end global hunger.

△ These Atlantic salmon are being farmed in Norway – 10 percent of seafood is farmed in this way. This figure is likely to triple by 2025.

▷ It is likely that droughts and famines will continue long into the 21st century. Millions of people, like these refugees in Zaire, will rely on food aid from other countries to survive.

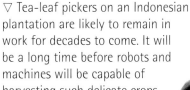

▽ Tea-leaf pickers on an Indonesian plantation are likely to remain in work for decades to come. It will be a long time before robots and machines will be capable of harvesting such delicate crops.

Unequal world

One of the great inequalities of the modern world is that, while some countries produce a surplus amount of food to their needs, millions still go hungry and die from starvation or malnutrition each year. However, this is likely to continue unless governments around the world take the initiative and there is a major shift in attitudes. It is also hoped that food production levels can be raised by biotechnology, advances in pest control and the creation of crops that can survive droughts and other extremes.

◁ In this greenhouse, a computer-controlled watering unit provides the exact amount of water required for optimum plant growth.

Popular science has often predicted that a person's nutritional needs could be contained in a single pill. Although it will soon be technically possible, the benefits and enjoyment of eating a variety of foods means that it is unlikely to become common.

▷ Killing pests such as slugs often involves chemical pesticides which leach into the soil. This pest-control robot can collect and eradicate pests without using chemicals. Once caught, the slugs are turned into biogas which powers the robot.

Farming fish

Fish and other products from the sea are a major source of protein. By 2015, worldwide demand for all forms of seafood is expected to increase by 50 percent. To fulfill this, the fishing industry will need to exploit new fishing grounds and invest more in aquaculture, or fish farming. Aquaculture takes place in lakes, ponds and reservoirs, where the environment can be carefully controlled.

Robo-farmers

Farming is time-consuming, labour-intensive work. In developed countries, farming is a mechanized process. A wide range of machines is used from combine-harvesters to crop-sorters and packaging devices in factories. Technology will continue to be developed in order to increase production for less cost. By 2025, robots will tend delicate greenhouse plants such as tomatoes, as well as harvesting fruit crops. More automation will also be used in the rearing of livestock.

▷ Hydroponics could become an important branch of farming. Hydroponics is the growing of plants without using soil. This researcher is studying lettuce and tomato plants in a laboratory in Arizona, USA.

◁▷ Biotechnology has the power to create uniquely patterned flowers as well as the potential for more important uses such as longer-lasting fruit and vegetables, or the creation of new drugs derived from plants or even animals.

BIOTECHNOLOGY

Biotechnology is the name given to a huge range of different industrial and agricultural processes that rely on the properties of living organisms. Although it is linked in many people's minds with genetic modification of plants and animals in order to create new hybrid species, this is only one part of the biotechnology story. Biotechnology has the potential to eradicate food shortages, cure many diseases and produce eco-friendly fuels and materials. However, the debate about whether we should be tampering with nature will continue for some time.

Food supplies

People have been selecting seeds, growing plant hybrids and inter-breeding animals for centuries to produce more robust crops and livestock. Biotechnology could lead to much greater yields from crops around the world. Damage inflicted by pests and diseases as well as spoiling at farms, packaging factories and stores mean that as much as half of all fruit and vegetables grown never becomes available to the consumer. By creating longer-lasting, disease-resistant products, food production could receive a massive boost by 2015.

△ A great part of biotechnology work on plants takes place in laboratories where genetically-engineered seedlings can be grown and studied in controlled conditions.

Growing plastics

Plants are likely to provide a major source of materials in the future. Ever since the 1920s, starch derived from plants has been used to produce acetone and paint solvents. One possibility is a new form of plastic that can be grown and stored within genetically modified plants such as potatoes. This type of plastic would not use up precious oil reserves and it would be cheap to produce. Furthermore, unlike most conventional plastics, it would also be biodegradable.

Medical breakthroughs

Biotechnology has the potential to make radical changes in the way we obtain many important drugs. Turnips have already been modified to produce anti-cancer drugs. Another developing strand of biotechnology called 'pharming' uses modified farm animals to generate important substances for the drugs industry. By 2025, 'pharmed' livestock may provide our most important medicines.

△ Advances in biotechnology have led to the first self-shearing sheep. The sheep is injected with a special solution called Bioclip which contains a protein that causes wool fibres to break away.

▷ A researcher analyses how a sweet sorghum plant reacts to different watering conditions. Sweet sorghum is a common cereal crop which scientists are studying to determine whether it can become a leading source of biofuel in the 21st century.

GENETIC ENGINEERING

Genes are the instructions that determine an organism's characteristics. In humans, for example, everything from hair and eye colour to susceptibility to certain diseases are passed down, or inherited, from parents via genes. Genes are contained in a chemical called DNA which is found in the cells of all living things. Identifying and understanding how to manipulate genes is beginning to revolutionize science. Genetic illnesses may one day become a thing of the past. Unborn children may be tested for genetic defects and treated in the womb using a technique called gene therapy. However, the ability to fundamentally alter genes, means that there are major concerns about the consequences of genetic engineering.

△ The British scientist Francis Crick and James Watson from the USA discovered·the double helix, or spiral, structure of DNA (deoxyribonucleic acid) in 1953. Two other scientists, Rosalind Franklin and Maurice Wilkins also played a crucial role.

Cloning

Scientists have been successful in creating identical copies, called clones, of existing plants and animals. In 1997, Dolly the sheep became the first mammal to be cloned from the cell of another adult. Cloning has given rise to fears of identical humans being created for sinister ends but it is far more likely to be used in medical research or to produce higher-yield crops.

◁ These baby mice glow green under a blue light. They have been genetically engineered to include a jellyfish gene that causes them to become fluorescent. The gene may be used to mark and study cancerous cells in humans.

◁ Dolly is a genetic duplicate, or clone. She was created from a cell extracted from an adult sheep.

▷ The Human Genome Project (HGP) is providing a new understanding of our genetic make-up. Four chemicals, known as A, G, C and T, are found in each gene. Determining their order is a major part of the HGP.

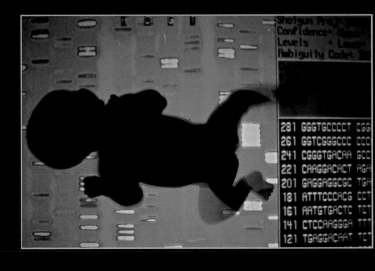

Shotgun
Confidence
Levels
Ambiguity Codes

281 GGGTGCCCCT CGG
261 GGTCGGGCCC CCC
241 CGGGTGACAA GCC
221 CAAGGACACT AGA
201 GAGGAGGCGC TGA
181 ATTTCCCACG CCT
161 AATGTGACTC TCT
141 CTCCAAGGGA TTT
121 TGAGGACAAT TCT

▷ The corkscrew-shaped DNA chemical is present in every single cell. DNA stores genes, which are the instructions that determine an organism's traits. Although it can only be seen under an electron microscope, human DNA would stretch almost five metres if it were unfolded.

△ Thousands of scientists are working across the world to determine the sequence of the coded information contained in human DNA.

▷ Special growth cells created by genetic engineering will play a major role in growing artificial skin and blood vessels.

Gene therapy

Genetic defects are responsible for almost 5,000 diseases. Gene therapy is a new form of treatment that involves the insertion of a healthy gene into a virus that has been neutralized so that it can do no harm. The modified virus, carrying the corrected gene, is then injected into the patient. In this way, inherited diseases including haemophilia and cystic fibrosis – the most common genetic disorder in the Western world – may be successfully combated.

CRYSTAL BALL

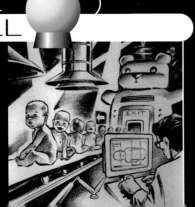

The power to manipulate the genes of unborn children raises the fear of 'designer' babies. In the future, unless prevented by law, parents will be able to specify the sex, looks and even the behaviour of their children.

Breaking the code

Begun in 1990, the Human Genome Project is one of the most ambitious and important scientific projects ever undertaken. Its main goal is to identify and map the 100,000 genes in human DNA. The Human Genome Project is expected to be completed before 2005. It will provide scientists with a revolutionary new tool for diagnosing, treating and, one day, potentially preventing most human diseases and disorders

◁ Many doctors once believed that protective clothing would prevent them catching their patients' illnesses. In the 1600s, doctors became known as 'quacks'. This came from the Dutch word 'quacksalver', a seller of remedies.

Historically, the world's biggest killers have not been wars or natural disasters, but diseases. In 1918, for instance, a new strain of influenza virus killed at least 40 million people. During the 20th century, average life expectancy across the globe increased as we learned more about diseases and how to combat them. Even so, in the first half of the 21st century medical research will face some major challenges. These will include the rise of certain diseases as populations age, and the possibility of new viruses and superbugs that are immune to conventional treatments.

FINDING A CURE

◁ A woman from northern India is injected with a vaccine against tetanus. Vaccinating people has been one of the greatest victories in the fight against disease.

△ The smart pill, unlike other oral medicines, will target a specific area of the body. After the pill has been swallowed, its path through the digestive system will be traced by radio signals. Once the pill has reached its destination (in this case a growth in the large intestine) a signal will be sent to release the drugs.

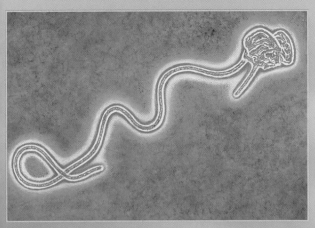

◁ The deadly Ebola virus, shown here at 19,000x magnification, is responsible for fever and, frequently, rapid death. Scientists must find new ways of treating such diseases. In many cases the overuse of antibiotics has created viruses that are drug-resistant.

Making the medicine go down

In the future, doctors will be able to tailor specific drug treatments for each patient with much greater effectiveness. Genetic testing will help determine exact dosages and reduce side effects. Some drugs will be sprayed onto edible strips of paper, while others will be dispensed via smart pills. Controlled by micro-electronics, smart pills will target a specific area of the body before releasing their cargo of drugs.

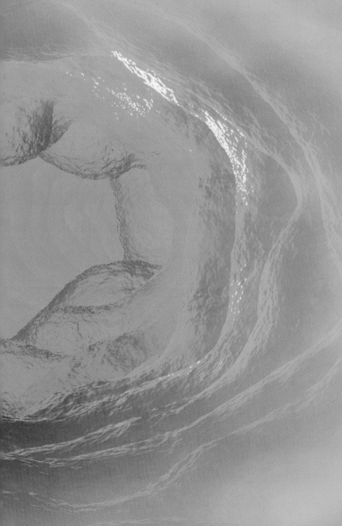

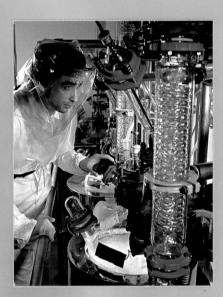

▷ Finding more effective ways of dispensing drugs is an important aspect of medical research. This technician is testing a drug that can be delivered by a simple spray system.

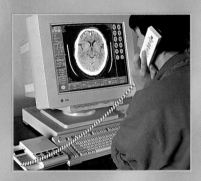

◁ A radiologist studies a brain scan of a patient which has been sent via a telephone line. Telemedicine will be used increasingly to allow specialists to make a diagnosis from almost anywhere in the world.

Screening

Preventive medicine and early diagnosis are the key to reducing the number of premature deaths. Today's PET and MRI scanners will be joined by even more powerful screening tools that can peer into the body and detect potential problems and diseases much earlier. These include laser probes that can identify pre-cancerous cells with extreme accuracy, and holographic medical imaging that will provide a three-dimensional view of the inside of the body.

Prevention

As life expectancy increases, so does the likelihood of developing certain diseases including many cancers, heart disease and diabetes. Our genetic make-up plays a major, but not exclusive, role in determining whether we become ill or not. During the 21st century there will be great emphasis on maintaining a healthy lifestyle in order to prevent disease. Diet, exercise and low stress levels will be promoted as the most important factors in staying healthy well into old age.

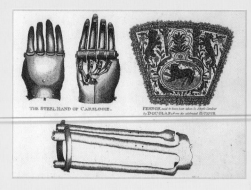

▷ During the 19th century, artificial limbs were very cumbersome and offered little flexibility. This 1815 engraving shows a steel hand and the metal frame that held it in place.

THE STEEL HAND OF CARSLOGIE.

REPAIRING OUR BODIES

△ It takes just three weeks to grow one square metre of artificial skin from a tiny fragment. Artificial skin is mainly used to help burns and other accident victims.

Until the second half of the 20th century, when people lost a limb, the most they could hope for was a crude, clumsy replacement. If a major internal organ such as the heart failed, then recovery was rare. Since the 1960s, there have been major advances in surgery, tissue engineering, artifical parts technology and transplant operations. These developments have saved millions of lives and improved the quality of life for countless others. Further breakthroughs will mean that by 2025, most of your body – both inside and out – can be repaired, or damaged parts replaced.

▷ Human cartilage cells have been grafted onto the back of a hairless mouse in an experiment to grow a replica of a human ear.

Robotic assistance
Robots are capable of much greater precision and accuracy than human hands and will play an increasingly important role in surgery. The majority of robots will work as surgical assistants, controlled by surgeons and theatre staff. By 2020, computer networks will allow surgeons to operate remotely by controlling a robot and other telesurgery machines from a distance.

Tissue engineering
Currently the demand for human body parts, especially internal organs, outstrips supply. This is set to change, however, with advances in tissue engineering. This branch of medical technology aims to create tissue and even new body parts from human cells. Scientists have already been successful in growing skin, pieces of bone and cartilage. Complete internal organs may be available by 2030. Known as neo-organs, these will be grown in laboratory conditions or even using animals as living hosts.

▷ The MRI scanner is a powerful body imaging system that has been of enormous benefit to surgery and body repair. MRI stands for Magnetic Resonance Imaging and produces detailed images of cross-sections of the human body.

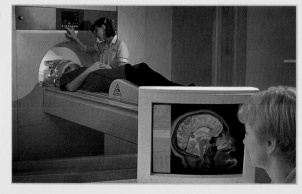

As we learn more about the sensory organs, there will be significant advances in the repair of impaired vision, speech and hearing. Eye transplants may be possible by 2030.

By 2040, major neo-organs such as the heart and lungs will be generated from cells. Tissues such as heart valves and blood vessels may be produced much sooner.

△ This robot helps pinpoint and treat diseased areas of the brain. A detailed three-dimensional computer image of the inside of the skull allows surgeons to control the robot and remove tumours with minimal damage to surrounding tissue.

Tissue engineering of body parts such as hands and ears will involve taking human cells and growing them over a three-dimensional scaffold made of biodegradable material. Fully functioning replacements could be in use by 2025.

Artificial hip and elbow joints are already made from incredibly strong metal alloys and composite materials.

◁ Advances in surgical techniques and tissue engineering mean that, with the likely exception of the brain, most body parts will become replaceable in the future.

△ The latest artificial legs contain microprocessors that help simulate the movement and response of a natural leg.

Running and many other activities are possible with the latest generation of artificial limbs. Scientists are currently experimenting with attaching them directly to nerves in order to restore feeling.

Bionic people

Science fiction has often featured people with bionic limbs and senses that exceed normal human abilities. By 2040, there may be a demand for high-performance parts that offer new levels of strength or precision. Bionic parts that enhance performance will probably be available only at a high price, and will inevitably cause much controversy.

◁ Until the 20th century, people across the world frequently died in childhood. In this painting from the 1880s, a mother tends to her sick daughter.

In the early 1900s, the average man or woman in the USA and Europe was not expected to live beyond the age of 45. A person born in a developed country at the start of the new millennium can hope to live for twice as long. Advances in medicine and improvements in diet and lifestyle have been and will continue to be the key to longer life expectancy. Research into our genetic make-up may even one day enable us to slow down the ageing process. For the forseeable future, however, the gap between life expectancy in developing nations and developed countries is likely to remain.

HOLDING
BACK THE YEARS

Rise of the old

An increasingly ageing population will have a profound effect on society. It is predicted that the number of post-retirement people will double by 2020, and that caring for the elderly will become one of the biggest industries. As people remain active for longer, society will find new ways to use their skills. Political parties may be formed to represent this growing and increasingly powerful section of the population.

The ageing process

Some scientists believe that there is a maximum age to which human beings can live. Others think that there is no natural limit and that locating the genes responsible for ageing in humans is the key to a much longer life. Scientists have successfully used genetic engineering to increase the length of life of simple organisms such as worms and fruit flies. But it is still much too early to tell if this will work in the far more complex human body.

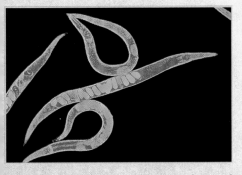

△ Nematode worms have been the focus of extensive research into genetic engineering. It has been shown that modified worms without a particular gene age more slowly than normal ones.

◁ In parts of Mongolia there is an unusually high proportion of people who are over 100 years old. Careful study of such people can help scientists to understand the connections between long life and lifestyle and, maybe one day, specific genes that control ageing.

Coming back from the dead

One possibility for defeating death is cryonics. This is the science of deep-freezing a person who has recently died in the hope that medical technology will be able to revive the corpse sometime in the future. Either the whole body or just the head is immersed in liquid nitrogen at absolute zero (-196°C) before the body tissue has had a chance to decay. One of the main challenges will be to restore a fully functioning brain with all its memories still intact.

▷ A number of people with fatal or terminal diseases have paid to be kept frozen in low-temperature capsules after they die. It is hoped that, sometime in the future, doctors will be able to revive and cure them.

▽ People live through three ages - childhood, adulthood and the third age (post-retirement). During the 21st century, as life expectancy increases, the number of post-retirement people will continue to rise.

GLOSSARY

Biotechnology The use of living organisms in industry, agriculture and science.

Cloning The process of creating copies of living things from a single cell without sexual reproduction taking place. The new copy, or clone, is physically and genetically identical to the parent cell.

Cloud-seeding The application of chemicals to clouds in order to generate rain.

Cryonics Preserving a dead person's body at low temperature, in the hope that future medical technology will be able to revive it.

Desalination The removal of salt and other minerals from sea water to create fresh water.

DNA A complex molecule, with a double-helix shape, that contains the genetic code for a living organism.

Gene therapy The identification and replacement of genes responsible for certain diseases with substitute healthy genes.

Genetic engineering The transfer of genes between species to create new organisms that do not occur naturally in nature.

Genome The sum total of DNA within a species.

Ground effect craft Vehicles, usually seacraft, that have wings to create extra lift. They skim at high speed across flat surfaces.

Hypersonic Term used for speeds above five times the speed of sound.

At sea level the speed of sound is 1,225 km/h.

Information Revolution
The massive changes in the ways people work and how information is handled brought on by improvements in computers and telecommunications.

Invasive surgery An operation on a patient that involves a large incision or cut being made so that the surgeon can see inside the area of the body to be operated upon.

Laser A highly-focused beam of light or other radiation, used to cut through objects, or to carry information through optical fibres.

Magnetic Levitation
A method of lifting objects by using magnetic attraction or the forces that keep magnets apart. Using a series of powerful magnets, it is possible for magnetic levitation to propel passenger-carrying trains at speeds of over 450 km/h.

Magnetohydrodynamic (MHD)
A new method of propulsion for sea craft. It uses superconducting magnets to generate a powerful electric field around thruster tubes filled with sea water.

Mass-transit systems Transport systems, such as underground tube trains, travelling walkways and bus networks that are designed to move large numbers of people.

Non-invasive surgery Surgery that relies on technology inserted through a small hole or holes into the patient's body.

Pharming The manufacture of medical products, particularly pharmaceutical drugs from genetically modified plants or

animals. Still in its infancy, this technology could lead to cheap medicines as well as products such as milk or plants that contain vaccines against human diseases.

Streamlining The designing and shaping of machines, particularly vehicles such as cars, boats and aircraft, so that they travel through the water or air more smoothly and efficiently.

Telesurgery The ability to send important medical information over a computer network so that a diagnosis can be made even though patient and doctor are in different places.

Teleworking Working from home and using technology such as computers, the Internet and fax machines to stay in touch with a central office and clients.

Tissue engineering The artificial creation of parts of the body using a variety of techniques.

Transgenic organism Any living organism that has had its genetic make-up manipulated and altered so that it includes one or more genes from a different species.

Virtual Reality A system that uses computers and senors to generate an artificial environment with which a human user can interact in a realistic way.

Virus A tiny organism that lives inside the cells of animals, plants and bacteria. Viruses can only reproduce inside cells and often cause diseases. In computing, a virus is a self-replicating computer program that often creates havoc by damaging other programs and erasing data in memory.

WEBSITES

There are thousands of websites that relate to technology in our lives. Here are a few of them:

Tomorrow's World, the long-running BBC programme, has a website that covers late-breaking news and in-depth features on 21st century technology. It can be found at: http://www.bbc.co.uk/tw/index.html

To see what a future house may look like both inside and out, visit:
http://users.netmatters.co.uk/dbb/fhouse.html

The exciting prospect of large numbers of ground effect vehicles is considered in detail at the following site:
http://www.io.tudelft.nl/~twaio/edwin/html/index.htm

Scientific American is a well-respected journal that reveals important scientific breakthroughs and makes future predictions. To explore the future of transport, medicine, weather prediction and food production, visit the magazine's website at: http://www.sciam.com/

The US magazine *Popular Science* examines the latest developments in technology and its impact. Its website can be found at: http://www.popsci.com

You can find out about advances in land, sea and air transport at: http://www.pbs.org/wgbh/nova/barrier

If you are interested in learning more about travel and transport, both in the present and the future, consider a visit to the biggest list of travel and transport-related links and resources on the Internet. They can be found at:
http://www.obd.nl/~otto/liste.htm

The one-stop centre if you want to learn more about the Human Genome Project is located at:
http://www.ornl.gov/TechResources/Human_Genome/home.html

The Wellcome Trust is the world's largest medical research charity. It has an extensive website which includes in-depth information on advances in medicine and biotechnology. You can find it at: http://www.wellcome.ac.uk

PLACES OF INTEREST

The Centre For Alternative Technology looks at sustainable, eco-friendly ways we can live our everyday lives in the future without damaging the planet. Alternative home design and energy use, innovative ways of using and recovering water and food production are all found at the centre, which is located at Powys in Wales.

Opening in September 2001, Birmingham's **Millennium Point** complex will include The University Of The First Age, an innovative learning facility for children and young people. There is also a major museum devoted to future technology in transport, at work and for leisure activities.

The Science Museum in London has over 40 individual galleries, many of which explore the past, present and future of technology.

Transport museums can be found all over the world. Amongst the most well-known are the **Henry Ford Motor Village** and the **National Air and Space Museum**, both in the USA. The latter museum, based in Washington, has many galleries devoted to both the history of space flight and exploration and displays on future developments.

Boasting over a million visitors a year, the **Singapore Science Centre** includes many interactive areas, including major exhibits on biotechnology and virtual voyages through the human body at the Centre's advanced Omni-theatre.

FURTHER READING

Futurewise by Patrick Dixon
(Harper Collins/1998)
Written by a specialist in future global trends, Patrick Dixon takes readers on a highly informative and fast-paced journey to the middle of the 21st century.

Visions by Michio Kaku
(Oxford University Press/1998)
A fascinating look at the key technologies, from artificial intelligence to genetic engineering, that will shape our lives during the 21st century and beyond.

INDEX

ACKNOWLEDGEMENTS

The publishers would like to thank the following illustrators
for their contribution to this book:

Julian Baum 10–11, 12–13, 30–31, 38–39, 54–55; Nik Clifford 3, 14–15,
28–29, 34–35, 36–37, 46–47, 49, 57; Graham Humphries 12, 25, 39, 53;
Dean McCallum 26–27; Mark Preston 6–7, 8–9,18–19, 32–33, 44–45,
50–51, 58–59; Real–Time Visualisation 16–17, 22–23.

The publishers would like to thank the following for supplying photoraphs:

Front cover bc SuperStock Ltd; 8 c Hulton Getty, cr Arcaid/Richard Bryant, bl Hulton Getty; 10 tl Mary Evans Picture Library, cl Science Photo Library/David Parker, bl Science Photo Library/M-Sat Ltd; 11 tc Science Photo Library/David Nunuk; 12 tl Mary Evans Picture Library, bc Still Pictures/Shehzad Nooran; 13 t Frank Spooner Pictures/Gamma, cr Arcaid/Ian Lambot, bc Mary Evans Picture Library; 14 tl Hulton Getty, bl Science Photo Library/George Olson; 15 TR Environmental Images/Martin Bond, br Frank Spooner Pictures/Gamma; 17 tl Science & Society Picture Library/Louis Hine/NMPFT, Bradford, cl Science Photo Library/David Parker, cr Science Photo Library/John Mead, br Frank Spooner Pictures/Auenturier; 18 l Mary Evans Picture Library, c Mary Evans Picture Library, cr Science & Society Picture Library/Science Museum, r Rex Features; 19 l Rex Features, cl Rex Features, cr Quadrant Picture Library; 20 tl Hulton Getty, br Rex Features/Peter Brooker; 20–21 c Rex Features; 21 tr Ford Motor Company, cr Quadrant Picture Library, br Vin Mag Archive Ltd; 22 t Hulton Getty, c Mercedes-Benz; 23 tl Rex Features, tr Rex Features, c Rex Features/Nils Jorgensen, b Frank Spooner Pictures/Gamma Liaison; 24 tl Mary Evans Picture Library, bl Robert Harding Picture Library/HP Merten, br Still Pictures/Hartmut Schwarzbach; 24–25 t Quadrant Picture Library; 26 t The Bridgeman Art Library/British Library; 27 t Solar Sailor, tl Rex Features, cl Tony Stone Images/Alastair Black, bc Rex Features, br Colorific/Paul Van Riel/Black Star; 28 tr Vin Mag Archive Ltd, bc Rex Features; 29 c British Airways, br Dennis Gilbert; 30 tl TRH, c Frank Spooner Pictures; 31 l Science Photo Library/Marshall Space Flight Center/NASA, r Martin Breeze/Retrograph Archive Ltd; 32 cl Science & Society Picture Library/Daily Herald Archive/NMPFT, c Rex Features, cr Rex Features, r Science & Society Picture Library/Science Museum; 34 tl Mary Evans Picture Library, bl Rex Features/Simon Hadley, bc Science Photo Library/Sam Ogden; 35 tl Tony Stone Images/Wayne R Bilenduke, bl Science Photo Library/James King-Holmes, br Rex Features; 36 tl Mary Evans Picture Library, cr Tony Stone Images/Walter Hodges, bl John Walmsley, BR Science Photo Library/Blair Seitz; 37 tr Camera Press/Stewart Mark; 38 tl Mary Evans Picture Library, cl Telegraph Colour Library/Jose Azel/Aurora; 39 TR Robert Harding Picture Library/Bill O'Connor, c Robert Harding Picture Library/Geoff Renner, br Planet Earth Pictures/Gary Bell; 40 tl Mary Evans Picture Library, bl Frank Spooner Pictures/Gamma presse images; 41 tl Allsport/Sylvain Cazenave, cr Katz Pictures/George Steinmetz/National Geographic Society; bc Rex Features; br Rex Features, 42 tl Mary Evans Picture Library/Barry Norman Collection, bl Allsport/Anne-Marie Weber; 42-43 c Rex Features, 43 tr Allsport/Didier Givois, br Allsport/Simon Bruty; 44 cr Science Photo Library/Laguna Design; 45 l Rex Features, cl Science & Society Picture Library/Science Museum, c Mary Evans Picture Library, br Science & Society Picture Library/Science Museum; 46 tl Mary Evans Picture Library, cl Rex Features/Pierre Schwartz/Sipa Press, bl Science Photo Library/Novosti Press Agency, br Science Photo Library/Simon Fraser; 47 tr Science Photo Library/David Ducros; 48 tr Hulton Getty, cl Still Pictures/Michel Roggo, cr Robert Harding Picture Library, b Still Pictures/Mark Edwards; 49 tl Still Pictures/Peter Frischmuth, tr Mary Evans Picture Library, b Science Photo Library/Peter Menzel; 50 c Science Photo Library/Tek Image; 51 tr Commonwealth Scientific and Industrial Research Organisation, c Science Photo Library/Tommaso Guicciardini; 52 tl Science Photo Library/A.Barrington Brown, c Science Photo Library/Makoto Iwafuji/Eurelios, bl Rex Features/Jeremy Sutton Hibbert, br Science Photo Library/Peter Menzel; 53 tl Still Pictures/Robert Holmgren, tr Science Photo Library/Laguna Design, c Science Photo Library/Peter Yates; 54 tl Mary Evans Picture Library, bl Science Photo Library/Simon Fraser; 55 tl Science Photo Library/Barry Dowsett, cl Science Photo Library/Simon Fraser, cr Science Photo Library/Geoff Tompkinson; 56 tr Mary Evans Picture Library/Webber, 1815, cl Science Photo Library/J.C. Revy, c BBC Photographic Library/Tomorrow's World, br Science Photo Library/ Geoff Tompkinson; 57 tr Science Photo Library/Klaus Guldbrandsen, bl Rex Features; 58 tl Mary Evans Picture Library; 59 tl Science Photo Library/James King-Holmes, tr Still Pictures/Adrian Arbib, ctr Frank Spooner Pictures/Gamma Liaison.

Key: b = bottom, c = centre, l=left, t = top, r = right

Every effort has been made to trace the copyright holders of the photographs. The publishers apologize for any inconvenience caused.

The publishers would like to thank the following: Kate Amy, Preston Carter, Sinead Derbyshire, Cormac Jordan, Malcolm Lee, Gerhardt Meurer of Johns Hopkins University, William Murray and Danny Wooton.